WHAT IS PROPAGANDA?

WAR DEPARTMENT EDUCATION MANUAL
EM-2
G. I. ROUNDTABLE SERIES

GREEN
POINT
BOOKS

Cover design
by Michael Schrauzer

This pamphlet is one of a series made available by the War Department under the series title *G. I. Roundtable.* As the general title indicates, *G. I. Roundtable* pamphlets provide material which orientation and education officers may use in conducting group discussions or forums as part of an off-duty education program.

The content of each pamphlet has been approved by the Historical Service Board of the American Historical Association.

Specific suggestions for the discussion or forum leader who plans to use this pamphlet will be found on page 43.

WAR DEPARTMENT
Washington 25, D. C., 4 July 1944

EM 2. *G. I. Roundtable: What Is Propaganda?* is published for the information of all concerned.
[A. G. 300.7 (4 July 44).]

BY ORDER OF THE SECRETARY OF WAR:
 G. C. MARSHALL,
  Chief of Staff.

OFFICIAL:
 J. A. ULIO.
  Major General,
   The Adjutant General.

DISTRIBUTION: X
(Additional copies should be requisitioned from USAFI, Madison. Wisconsin, or nearest Overseas Branch.)

WHAT IS
PROPAGANDA?

DEFINING PROPAGANDA

An attempt to define propaganda is made near the end of this pamphlet *after* we have examined its main characteristics, In order to avoid mistaken ideas, however, it may be useful to point out at once what some of these characteristics are.

Propaganda isn't an easy thing to define, but most students agree that it has to do with *any ideas or beliefs that are intentionally propagated.*

It uses words and word substitutes in trying to reach a goal—pictures, drawings, graphs, exhibits, parades, songs, and other devices.

Of course propaganda is used in controversial matters, but it is also used to promote things that are generally acceptable and noncontroversial.

So there are different kinds of propaganda. They run all the way from selfish, deceitful, and subversive effort to honest and aboveboard promotion of things that are good.

Propaganda can be concealed or open, emotional or containing appeals to reason, or a combination of emotional and logical appeals.

Turn to page 46 for a fuller discussion of "Defining Propaganda."

WHAT IS
PROPAGANDA?

I T IS THE SPRING OF 1940. ALLIED armies face the German columns, but there is little action at the front, and a group of French soldiers find time to listen to an enemy broadcast.

"Where are the English?" asks the radio voice. The enemy broadcaster is speaking in French. The soldiers listen uneasily.

"I'll tell you where your English comrades are," continues the voice. "They lounge about Paris and fill the night clubs. Have you seen a Tommy in the Maginot Line? Of course not. French soldiers, you will find the Tommies behind the lines — with your wives."

Propaganda. Of course. The German propaganda strategy of division, intended to sow suspicion and doubt about the fidelity of an ally. The propaganda preparatory to the blitz.

A handful of Londoners are drinking ale in their neighborhood pub. The time is July 1940. The French have signed Hitler's armistice terms, but Britain is still holding out. The pub keeper turns the dials of the tavern radio to tune in on "Lord Haw-Haw," the Berlin broadcaster, and the voice booms out:

"England is ripe for invasion.... You might as well expect help from an army of mastodons as from the United States.... You are on a doomed ship.... Whether or not the people of Britain want to see their fields turned into graveyards and their cities into tombs is a matter for themselves and Mr. Churchill. Perhaps if the British people could speak, they would ask for peace. But since the official voice of England asks not for peace but for destruction, it is destruction we must provide."

The propaganda of fear. The voice of defeatism.

It is the autumn of 1941. The United States is still neutral, but an American Army is in training, a Navy is being strengthened, and Lend-Lease supplies are crossing the Atlantic.

An American sits at home tinkering with his short-wave set and he picks up an English-language broadcast beamed to North America from Germany.

"The German government and the German people have only the friendliest of feelings for the United States, the home of so many American citizens of German descent." The words of the radio speaker are honeyed words. "Let it be said for once and all," the broadcaster continues, "that a German victory in this war is no threat to English democracy — and certainly not to American democracy."

The propaganda voice of appeasement. Here is the strategy of attempting to hypnotize a people with an assertion of the "peaceful intentions" of the Nazi war machine.

In a few brief months the Japs strike at Pearl Harbor, and the Germans declare war against those for whom they said they cherished "only the friendliest of feelings."

ENEMY PROPAGANDA

Hitler is the arch propagandist of our time. These are examples of his strategy in attempting to mold the opinions and attitudes of his intended victims to his own purposes. Division, doubt, and fear are the weapons he uses within one nation and among Allied countries arrayed against him. His purpose is summed up in his own phrase — to sow "mental confusion, contradiction of feeling, indecision, panic."

Since Hitler's propaganda is a weapon constantly used against us, we need to understand clearly his techniques and devices — not only those he employs today, but also the cunning and diabolical methods by which he and his Brown Shirts combined propaganda and other pressures, first to take over the German state, then to stamp out all vestiges of freedom in it. The story goes back to the early 1920's.

The very name of the party headed by Hitler was chosen with great deliberation for its propaganda effect. The little group of fanatical men who called themselves the German Labor Party in 1919 later sought a name that would have widespread appeal. Hitler and his adherents chose "National Socialist German Workers' Party," reduced by popular usage to "Nazi." Each word of this title had a special significance for certain groups in Germany. "Socialist" and "National," for example, were associated with causes that long antedated Hitler. That was what Hitler wanted — a name that would prove a catchall, an omnibus upon which many could ride.

The Nazi banner was a product of Hitler's contriving. He hated the black, red, and gold flag of the German Republic against which he was conspiring. Since the old imperial colors of the days of the kaiser could still arouse powerful emotions, he decided he must use some of the colors of this old banner — black, white, and red. In 1920 Hitler and his followers made up a striking flag with the hooked cross or swastika dominant, but with the colors that would capture the allegiances of various groups of Germans — red to capture Socialist sentiment and white to appeal to the Nationalists. The black swastika within the white circle is a symbol of the anti-Semitic platform of the Nazi leader and his fanatical supporters.

The Nazi salute — the upraised arm — was a device created to identify party members and the Nazi movement. Further identification was given through the use of the party salutation, "Heil Hitler," and as time went on both members and nonparty Germans used it. Then came the invention of party slogans — *Blut und Boden* (Blood and Soil), and others that have a strange ring on democratic ears but which appealed to the followers of "the leader."

Hitler hypnotized the German people by staging dramatic parades and gigantic and spectacular rallies and demonstrations. One department of the Nazi propaganda office spent all its time planning rallies, selecting badges, emblems, uniforms, costumes, flags, and "background" effects to give glitter to the assemblages. While marching men and massed bands incited party delegates, the ritualistic ceremonies and the emotional speeches of the leader stirred Nazi members into a further frenzy.

As an example of how mass propaganda was organized, look at a typical Nuremberg party rally. The participants or actors numbered 110,000 storm troopers, 50,000 labor servicemen and women, 180,000 party officials, and 120,000 ordinary party members—a total of 460,000, equal to thirty army divisions. Visitors numbering 550,000 looked on at the ceremonies.

These techniques were deliberately designed, as one propaganda expert points out, "to bring about identification of larger and larger numbers with first, the Nazi cause, and then with what, after they gained power, was termed the 'true national community.'"

After they captured office, the Nazis were ruthless in stamping out all vestiges of the German Republic. The symbols of the Führer and the Nazi party became preeminent. The so-called "leadership principle" which exalted Hitler into an infinitely wise, an almost god-like, chieftain was one of the fictions created by his adherents.

The Nazis established a ministry of propaganda. They licensed and catalogued German newspapermen to keep them in control, suppressed or "integrated" unfriendly newspapers, and as the crisis developed in Europe, expelled foreign correspondents who sought to tell the truth of what went on in Germany. They took over the broadcasting system and every other agency that bore a relationship to the cultural life of the people.

But despite all Nazi cunning, the propaganda tricks and the creation of dazzling new symbols could not take the minds of the German people entirely off their troubles. The Nazis then cleverly drained away some of these resentments by finding scapegoats — minority groups against whom blame for difficulties could be charged. The trade unions were one scapegoat, the Versailles Treaty another, the Communists a third, and the democracies a fourth. But the Jew was the easiest target. The German people could blame all these "enemies" for their own state of affairs and thus seem to free themselves of fault.

Against the Jews, the Nazis turned their wrath. The Jew, they said, was not an "Aryan." They claimed that he had "sold out" the Germans in World War I. He was in league, they charged, with "international capitalism." They held him to be the chief cause of inflation in Germany. In a word, they accused him of causing most of the ills from which the nation suffered. They heaped their troubles on his head. The "non-Aryan" myth fitted into the dogma of the racial superiority of the Germanic stock, one of the fictions spread by the Nazi party "philosophers."

The club and pistol, concentration camp, and secret police were the means of putting down the Jews and other minority groups whenever propaganda by itself was not enough. To the weapons of propaganda and censorship, the Nazis had added a third — terror.

Germany became a nation built upon propaganda, plus force. The political state became the shadow of the Nazi party.

After establishing the dictatorship in 1933-34, Hitler used his energies for a time in fastening the Nazi yoke on the necks of the German people. The next step was to prepare the ground in countries that he wished to annex or control. Paul Joseph Goebbels, head of the propaganda ministry, got unlimited funds and authority to foment trouble among Germany's neighbors. Here again propaganda was combined with terror. Uniting propaganda with threats, veiled bribes, subversive tactics, and outright violence, the Nazis "softened up" Austria and the Sudetenland for the "kill." By propaganda and other means, they weakened France through stirring up class conflicts within the French Republic. Using similar methods, they forced minor states to submit to dictation from Berlin.

The Nazis have never disguised their lack of principles. Eugen Hadamowski, a Goebbels assistant, once said, "The use of force can be a part of propaganda." The idea was first, to confuse and strike fear into the hearts of your own countrymen, and then to use similar techniques to demoralize the people of other countries. Here is the plan the Nazis used in their propaganda warfare against former friends and neighbors:

Nazi strategists sought out the "soft spots" in the areas they planned to absorb or attack. Rival economic interests, racial and religious antagonisms, tensions between political groups, cleavages between workers and employers — these were studied in every detail. If, in the nation about to be attacked, influential persons were discovered who could be bribed or corrupted, German agents made use of these quislings. In a careful index, German espionage services charted possible approaches to key politicians, businessmen, military leaders and others — knew their habits, peculiarities, even their vices. Every political faction was analyzed for its possible usefulness to Germany.

Then Nazi agents built up in the victim country a front of discontented elements who could be managed in times of crisis. Thus the rancors, grudges, and disloyalties of these elements would serve to divide a nation and destroy its unity. Every country has groups of discredited political figures, demagogues, extreme reactionaries, misguided idealists, and die-hards who can be misled by glittering promises. Play our game, the Nazis told some of these groups, and we will elevate you to positions of power and influence.

THEY PRETEND FRIENDSHIP—THEN GIVE THEM "THE WORKS"

Another technique was to pretend friendship for the country against which force was to be used while secretly plotting its destruction. While a peaceful neighbor slumbered, hoping the German propagandists really meant what they said, the Nazis perfected their plans. When disunity, stimulated by Nazi underground tactics, developed, however, Germany grew bolder. Hitler then made threats and demands. Goebbels echoed his master. The Nazi propaganda machine issued a barrage describing the great strength of the German army and air force and the folly of even trying to resist them. Nazi attacks discredited the doomed country's leaders, no matter how honest and sincere those leaders were. The "war of nerves" was unleashed. The Nazis were then ready to strike.

All this required careful preparation and the cynical union of propaganda and terror. Before attacks were made on Austria, Czechoslovakia, Poland, Norway, the Netherlands, or France, the Nazis planted their subversive agents in legations, consulates, and tourist bureaus, created Nazi party "cells" within a country's borders, and established espionage services which ramified all over the world. Treacherous persons already in the pay or under the influence of the Nazis—the "fifth columnists"—were ready to "sell out" when the time came for the Nazis to strike.

That was the technique of the "invasion from within" and the propaganda attack from without. That was the means used to crush a nation even before the tramp of German soldiers rang in the streets of invaded cities.

I'LL MAKE UP MY OWN MIND!

DEMOCRATIC VS.
ENEMY PROPAGANDA

Hitler and his partners in aggression are not the only experts in propaganda, however. The weapon of propaganda in the modern world must be parried and the blows returned by counter-propaganda. In the struggle for men's minds that is constantly being waged by propagandists there is, however, a fundamental difference between the propaganda of dictatorship and the propaganda of democracy.

Hitler himself, in *Mein Kampf*, laid down his rules for dictatorship. He stated the "principle of the whopping lie" and of the gullibility

DER FÜHRER IS ALWAYS RIGHT!

of the masses. If you are going to tell a lie, he said, and nobody doubts that he intended to, don't tell a little one, because it will be recognized as a lie. Tell the biggest and most unlikely lie you can think of, keep on telling it, and the people will think it must be the truth and believe it. "The greater the lie, the more effective it is as a weapon," said the master of the alleged "master race."

Moreover, he went on, don't be fooled into thinking that you have to sway the influential people — the leaders of opinion — to your side first. "Toward whom must propaganda be directed," he asked, "toward the scientific intelligentsia or toward the uneducated masses?" His answer was, "It must always and exclusively be directed toward the masses. The teachability of the great masses is very limited, their understanding small, and their memory short." In a word, he believes that it pays to take advantage of ignorance and that it is therefore best to keep the people ignorant.

Democracy is a different kind of system from the ground up. It is based on the people, and it works well in proportion as the people are enlightened and informed about what goes on both in peace and in war (though of course democratic people recognize the wisdom of some wartime censorship imposed for security reasons). This basic democratic principle was stated by President George Washington in his Farewell Address when he said, "In proportion as the structure of a government gives force to public opinion, it is essential that public opinion should be enlightened." To the degree that people are denied access to the facts and to a wide range of independent interpretations of the facts, democracy fails to function effectively.

These simple truths determine the underlying or governing principles of democratic propaganda. The Nazis blindfold their people against the truth. In exact opposition to the rules of Hitler, the democratic countries must present the truth in their propaganda. A free people will soon find out the truth in spite of official suppressions and distortions. And when propaganda has been revealed to be deceitful and distorted, it no longer is effective. Moreover, democratic propaganda must observe the right of the people to know the facts, however unpleasant they may be. The strategy of truth is not only in accord with the basic principles of democracy, but is also a hardheaded and realistic policy for effective dealing with allies, neutrals, and even enemies.

WAR PROPAGANDA

The Nazis prepared for war from the moment Hitler came into power in 1933. In the feverish building up of German striking power, they had the support of the professional military men. The Nazis not only produced the weapons of war; they geared their economy for the strain of a future conflict. They carried on political intrigues to promote their purposes. Their propaganda machine had long been a going concern when Hitler felt ready to strike at Poland, the first step in an ambitious plan to lay the world at his feet.

Military, economic, political, and propaganda weapons were forged for the fray. Britain and France and, soon after, other peaceful nations were compelled to forge them to resist the Nazi onrush.

Today's war is four-dimensional. It is a combination of military, economic, political, and propaganda pressure against the enemy. An appeal to force alone is not regarded as enough, in the twentieth century, to win final and lasting victory. War is fought on all four fronts at once — the military front, the economic front, the political front, and the propaganda front.

To understand how this four-dimensional warfare has come about, we have to look at history. We have to go back to the rise of nationalism in the eighteenth century.

Before the American and French revolutions took place at the end of the eighteenth century, many armies fought in the pay of monarchies, such as the Bourbons, Hapsburgs, and Hohenzollerns, or of individual leaders. They were mercenary armies. They did not fight for patriotic motives. They did not fight for causes. They fought because fighting was their business. No fight, no pay!

Something new came when the Americans formed a citizen army to win their independence and when the French threw off the yoke of the Bourbons. The French raised a national army to beat back the Austrians and Prussians who were seeking to choke off the new French state. These Frenchmen were fighting for France, for the country they loved. They weren't fighting for a despot, a royal house, or money. Like the Americans, they were fighting for their country.

About the same time, the Industrial Revolution was introducing a vital change in the methods of warfare. Larger and larger production became possible because of machinery. New mechanized forms of weapons came into use. Today's sequel of this story is seen in airplanes, tanks, landing boats, aircraft carriers, and a thousand other modern instruments of war.

One result of this change is that modern war calls for large armies in the field. Where 1 per cent of the population was once considered a large number to call to the colors, 10 per cent can now be mobilized. And populations are much bigger than they used to be. But modern war means not only big armies in the field. It also means even bigger civilian armies back of them, on the home front. For every man in the field, we are told, there must be a half-dozen workers in the factories and fields at home. So the masses of men directly engaged in modern war effort are staggering.

There are other changes, too. Today's great accumulation of capital means that war can be waged on a large scale and for long periods. The mechanization of armies and navies means not only that the actual battle front can cover thousands of miles, where in the past the battle area was relatively small, but also that fighting men can continue a campaign, without stopping, through a Russian winter, a Burmese rainy season, or an African summer.

PROMOTION OF A WORTH-WHILE

The result of these changes is that propaganda has become in modern war not only a formidable weapon against the enemy but likewise a necessary tool in promoting a national war effort. Through it are carried popular appeals to make the necessary sacrifices and to contribute muscle, mind, and money to the successful prosecution of the war. In a democratic country, under governments chosen by and responsible to the people, the entire population, in and out of uniform, must be informed of the progress of the war. A free flow of information serves to stimulate the war effort, strengthens the nation to stand reverses, to hold steadfast through a long conflict, to take losses courageously, to make sacrifices bravely, to buy bonds generously, and to cooperate in every way possible in the great national effort for victory.

The political aspects of war tie in closely with all this, as has been shown, for

CAUSE IS GOOD PROPAGANDA . . .

example, by the Moscow, Cairo, and Teheran conferences. The combatant nations must have programs for victory and programs for peace. And their people must be told about them.

But even that isn't the whole story. Propaganda in wartime must seek to demoralize enemy morale. A primary objective of propaganda aimed at enemy nations is to break down their will to fight. It seeks to lower the enemy's will to resist and it does this in several ways. One is to picture the military successes on the propagandist's side. Another is to picture the armed might and economic power that the enemy has to face. Yet another is to picture the moral superiority of the cause against which the enemy is fighting. It is part of a nation's strategic plan to intimidate enemy leaders, to separate them from their people, and to break down resistance by producing evidence that the mass of the enemy people have been deceived and misled.

Propaganda, too, is an instrument for maintaining unity and good will among allies banded together in a common effort. It is sometimes effective in bringing opinion in neutral states over to one side or another. And in the battle zones it serves to keep up the morale of the men who are doing the actual fighting job.

So, as you contrast the tremendous volume and intensity of war propaganda today with the situation in wars of other eras, you can't escape the conclusion that what is going on now is a modern phenomenon. Propaganda of some sort had, it is true, been used in warfare for centuries. But all the social, economic, industrial, and military factors that make propaganda a large-scale part of war in 1944 first made themselves seriously felt in World War I. In that war, propaganda for the first time became an important and formal branch of government. It is in modern times that we have become familiar with such governmental institutions as the British Ministry of Information, the German Ministry of Propaganda and Public Enlightenment, the American Committee on Public Information (in World War I), the Office of War Information (in World War II), and their counterparts in many other countries.

TRUTH TELLING PROMOTES GOOD WILL AMONG ALLIES

It should not be forgotten that the astonishing forward strides in communications in the twentieth century have had a lot to do with the development of propaganda—especially radio broadcasting. Not only is propaganda vital to the conduct of modern war; it is also possible to reach many millions of people regularly, day and night, who only twenty-five years ago might have been almost beyond the reach of propaganda. Not only the words but the actual voices of the leaders of the nations at war are familiar to millions of people the world over, carried by the magic of radio.

THE STORY OF PROPAGANDA

The fact that wars give rise to intensive propaganda campaigns has made many persons suppose that propaganda is something new and modern. The word itself came into common use in this country as late as 1914, when World War I began. The truth is, however, that propaganda is not new and modern. Nobody would make the mistake of assuming that it is new if, from early times, efforts to mobilize attitudes and opinions had actually been called "propaganda." The battle for men's minds is as old as human history.

In the ancient Asiatic civilization preceding the rise of Athens as a great center of human culture, the masses of the people lived under despotisms and there were no channels or methods for them to use in formulating or making known their feelings and wishes as a group. In Athens, however, the Greeks who made up the citizen class were conscious of their interests as a group and were well informed on the problems and affairs of the city-state to which they belonged. Differences on religious and political matters gave rise to propaganda and counter-propaganda. The strong-minded Athenians, though lacking such tools as the newspaper, the radio, and the movies, could use other powerful engines of propaganda to mold attitudes and opinions. The Greeks had games, the theater, the assembly, the law courts, and religious festivals, and these gave opportunity for propagandizing ideas and beliefs. The Greek playwrights made use of the drama for their political, social, and moral teachings. Another effective instrument for putting forward points of view was oratory, in which the Greeks excelled. And though there were no printing presses, handwritten books were circulated in the Greek world in efforts to shape and control the opinions of men.

RADIOS ARE THE EARS OF THE "UNDERGROUND." THEIR PRESSES PASS THE GOOD WORD ALONG.

From that time forward, whenever any society had common knowledge and a sense of common interests, it made use of propaganda. And as early as the sixteenth century nations used methods that were somewhat like those of modern propaganda. In the days of the Spanish Armada (1588), both Philip II of Spain and Queen Elizabeth of England organized propaganda in a quite modern way.

On one occasion, some years after the Spanish Armada, Sir Walter Raleigh complained bitterly about the Spanish propaganda (though he didn't use that name). He was angry about a Spanish report of a sea battle near the Azores between the British ship *Revenge* and the ships of the Spanish king. He said it was "no marvel that the Spaniard should seek by false and slanderous pamphlets, advisoes, and letters, to cover their own loss and to derogate from others their own honours, especially in this fight being performed far off." And then he recalled that back at the time of the Spanish Armada, when the Spaniards "purposed the invasion" of England, they published "in sundry languages, in print, great victories in words, which they pleaded to have obtained against this realm; and spread the same in a most false sort over all parts of France, Italy, and elsewhere." The truth of course was that the Spanish Armada suffered a colossal disaster in 1588.

The Spanish claims, though described in the language of Queen Elizabeth's time, have a curiously modern ring. Make a few changes in them, here and there, and they sound like a 1944 bulletin from the Japanese propaganda office.

The term "propaganda" apparently first came into common use in Europe as a result of the missionary activities of the Catholic church. In 1622 Pope Gregory XV created in Rome the Congregation for the Propagation of the Faith. This was a commission of cardinals charged with spreading the faith and regulating church affairs in heathen lands. A College of Propaganda was set up under Pope Urban VIII to train priests for the missions.

In its origins "propaganda" is an ancient and honorable word. Religious activities which were associated with propaganda commanded the respectful attention of mankind. It was in later times that the word came to have a selfish, dishonest, or subversive association.

Throughout the Middle Ages and in the later historic periods down to modern times, there has been propaganda. No people has been without it. The conflict between kings and Parliament in England was a historic struggle in which propaganda was involved. Propaganda was one of the weapons used in the movement for American independence, and it was used also in the French

Revolution. The pens of Voltaire and Rousseau inflamed opposition to Bourbon rule in France, and during the revolution Danton and his fellows crystallized attitudes against the French king just as Sam Adams and Tom Paine had roused and organized opinion in the American Revolution.

Propaganda was used in the movement for American independence

World War I dramatized the power and triumphs of propaganda. And both fascism and communism in the postwar years were the centers of intense revolutionary propaganda. After capturing office, both fascists and communists sought to extend their power beyond their own national borders through the use of propaganda.

In our modern day, the inventive genius of man perfected a machinery of communication which, while speeding up and extending the influence of information and ideas, gave the propagandists a quick and efficient system for the spread of their appeals. This technical equipment can be used in the interests of peace and international good will.

WE ARE NOW RETURNING BLOW FOR BLOW

Hitler, Mussolini, and Tojo preferred to seize upon this magnificent nervous system for selfish ends and inhumane purposes, and thus enlarged the role of propaganda in today's world. While the United Nations were slow at first to use the speedy and efficient devices of communication for propaganda purposes, they are now returning blow for blow.

The modern development of politics was another stimulus to propaganda. Propaganda as *promotion* is a necessary part of political campaigns in democracies. When political bosses controlled nominations, comparatively little promotion was needed before a candidate was named to run for office, but under the direct primary system the candidate seeking nomination must appeal to a voting constituency. And in the final election he must appeal to the voters for their verdict on his fitness for office and on the soundness of his platform. In other words, he must engage in promotion as a legitimate and necessary part of a political contest.

In democracies, political leaders in office must necessarily explain and justify their courses of action to an electorate. Through the use of persuasion, those in office seek to reconcile the demands of various groups in the community. Prime ministers, presidents, cabinet members, department heads, legislators, and other officeholders appeal to the citizens of community and nation in order to make a given line of policy widely understood and to seek popular acceptance of it.

In peacetime the promotional activities of democratic governments usually consist of making the citizens aware of the services offered by a given department and of developing popular support for the policies with which the department is concerned. The purpose is to make these services "come alive" to the everyday citizen, and in the long run official information and promotion tend to make the average man more conscious of his citizenship. If the public is interested in the work done in its name and in its behalf, intelligent public criticism of governmental services can be stimulated.

Recent economic changes have expanded the volume of propaganda. Under the conditions of mass production and mass consumption, techniques of propaganda and public relations have been greatly developed to help sell commodities and services and to engender good will among consumers, employees, other groups, and the public at large.

WHAT ARE THE TOOLS OF PROPAGANDA?

Whether the propagandist works in a peacetime or wartime situation, he uses certain tools to mobilize opinions and attitudes. What are these tools?

An important one is *suggestion*. Another word for it is *stimulation*.

The propagandist tries to *stimulate* others to accept without challenge his own assertions, or to act as he wants them to do. The idea of using *suggestion* or *stimulation* as a propaganda device is that it will lead a public to accept a proposition even though there are not logical grounds for accepting it. The propagandist usually tries to sidestep critical reactions from his audience, and therefore suggestion is one of his most important tools.

How does the propagandist use this tool? By making broad and positive statements.

By presenting his statements in simple and familiar language. By refusing to admit, or even suggest, that there is another side to the question. Hitler's brutal and direct suggestion that the Jews sold out the German people in World War I — the "stab in the back," the Nazi propagandists called it — is an example of this kind of propaganda. Another example is the repeated Nazi propagandist assertion that Prime Minister Churchill and President Roosevelt are "warmongers."

Suggestion is a highly developed art in commercial advertising. An obvious example is the flat declaration that some brand of vitamin will remedy "that tired and run-down feeling."

A second propaganda tool is only a subtler form of suggestion. This tool is the use of hints, insinuations, or indirect statements.

An example or two from the field of advertising will illustrate this method. The sponsorship of a symphony orchestra by a commercial company may be expected to create a feeling of good will on the part of the listener toward the product of the sponsor. Sometimes programs designed to portray the life and culture of another country are propagandistic in nature, designed to "sell" that country to listeners in a home country.

A third method of propaganda is the appeal to the known *desires* of an audience. Psychologists say that desire is an important factor in belief. Thus some persons may support some unsound economic scheme because they desire an income in their old age. Others will subscribe to some fraudulent "scheme of psychology" in order to improve their "personality."

The self-interested propagandist will study public opinion to find out what things people are "for" or "against" in order to decide on the labels that he will use to bring about desired reactions. He knows that such words as "justice," "Constitution," "Americanism," and "law and order," which arouse favorable attitudes, will serve as a favorable background for his message, and so he uses them. On the other hand, he may use certain other words — for example, "radical" or "un-American" — to influence his listeners to reject a cause or idea that he regards as inimical to his own interests,

Hitler is adept and completely unscrupulous in appealing to various groups in Germany. There has been little consistency in his appeals, but there have been many suggested cure-alls for discontented or unhappy groups. The insincerity of the Nazi performance is revealed in the statement of a careful student who says, "National Socialism has no political or social theory. It has no philosophy and no concern for the truth. In a given situation it will accept any theory that might prove useful; and it will abandon that theory as soon as the situation changes...."

National Socialism is for agrarian reform and against it, for private property and against it, for idealism and against it."

The advertising man appeals to desire in the interest of his client. The desire to be strong and healthy, to be socially acceptable, to be beautiful, sells drug products, cosmetics, reducing preparations, soaps, perfumes. Anyone who is accustomed to reading advertisements will instantly recall dozens of illustrations of appeals to such desires used to promote a wide variety of products.

The skilled propagandist also knows the techniques of "making ideas stick." It is because of this knowledge that he resorts to key words and slogans, shibboleths, or other symbolic forms.

The advertising slogan packs meaning into short sentences. The purpose is to get them noticed. They will find their way into the minds of people. When a person is choosing a commodity to buy, it is expected that the slogan will come easily to the surface of his mind. A good many years ago advertisers discovered that "reason-why" appeals were not always effective. Appeals were shortened and emotionalized, since many readers will not wade through explanations of why one commodity is better than another.

The history of international political propaganda, the experts tell us, is full of examples of the use of striking slogans. For example, "the sick man of the Golden Horn" was used as a description of the former Turkish Empire. In Hitler's name-calling techniques, the democratic nations are called "pluto-democracies." While seeking power he used the campaign cry: "The Versailles Treaty is a monstrous lie." Under Mussolini, the Fascists were fond of such slogans as "a book and a rifle make a perfect Fascist" and "a plough makes a furrow but a sword defends it."

Though the Nazi propaganda both inside and outside Germany has been marked by terror, this is not a common characteristic of slogans and symbols. No one could challenge such Red Cross slogans as "All you need is a heart and a dollar." No one could question the socially minded impulse behind the Salvation Army slogan, "A man may be down but he's never out." Compelling slogans have been devised to win support for war relief, community help, and many other such activities,

Sometimes slogans have fired the imaginations of people in the past and continued their influence down to the present. One authority suggests that if a slogan catches correctly and objectively "the underlying forces in a critical situation," it may turn out to be "vital and lasting." We remember such striking slogans as "No Taxation without Representation" from the American Revolution, "Liberty, Equality, and Fraternity" from the French Revolution, and "Peace, Bread, and Land" from the Russian Revolution.

Propaganda makes use of slogans, but it also makes effective use of symbols. A symbol is a concrete representation of an idea, action, or thing — a sign that stands for something, as crossed rifles stand for the Infantry and as wings and propeller represent the Air Forces.

A symbol can be a word, a mark, an object, a song, a flag, an image, a picture, a statue, or some collective or grouped representation — anything that conveys a common thought to masses of people. A symbol is a kind of cement that holds together a social group.

The propagandist knows the art of working with symbols. He uses symbols to develop both favorable and unfavorable attitudes.

Symbol usage will create likenesses that are used much as a stenographer uses shorthand. Cartoonists have stereotyped symbols to represent the taxpayer, the college professor, and many others. One cartoonist pictured the "prohibitionist" as a tall, thin, long-nosed, black-garbed figure in a plug hat, and others portrayed the saloonkeeper as a very fat, barrel-like figure. The "capitalist" was once pictured as a huge diamond-studded man wearing a suit covered with dollar signs.

There is some reason to believe that in the past half century there has been a decrease in the number of popular symbols used in the Western nations. But a vast amount of symbolism has been created by the fascist, Nazi, and communist states.

The Nazis made their symbols so unmistakable and conspicuous that if any German omitted to display or use them, he would be quickly detected. These symbols, you will recall, included the Nazi salute, the swastika, and a lot of titles, badges, and uniforms. "Hitler himself," writes one authority, "must have his own title, denied by special edict to all other leaders, and he won great popular approval, after the death of Hindenburg, by pretending that the title President was altogether too august for him."

The use of "non-Aryan" as a symbol by Hitler and the Nazi hierarchy was a demagogic device to encourage the persecution of minority scapegoats who were neither numerous nor powerful enough to resist the violent tactics of the Nazi propagandists and Nazi terrorists.

Catchwords and slogans abound in Nazi propaganda, contrived for the sake of impressing the German people. The Nazis are fond of such important and high-sounding words and phrases as "immutable," "imperishable," and "for all future time." Opportunists, they are quick to discard a slogan when it has served its purpose. Then new ones are coined and must be on all German lips.

The chief symbol used to inspire the Japanese civilian and fighting man is the emperor. The Japanese higher-ups maintain their internal power by making a god of their emperor — emphasizing his alleged descent from the sun god. This symbol of the emperor as god is used to stimulate the fighting effectiveness of soldiers and sailors. The Japanese, in their propaganda attacks on Americans and British, play up the symbol "white exploiter." They disguise Japanese imperialism behind the symbol of "co-prosperity" in their efforts to win converts among the brown and yellow races.

Another technique used by the propagandist is the prestige element in human relations.

The psychologists are not agreed as to the extent to which attitudes and opinions can be propagated by prestige, but it seems certain that prestige does play an important role. The influence the parent has over his child, for example, can be traced in part to the prestige of an adult — in size, strength, knowledge, and power.

Some individuals or groups resent expert opinion and are unwilling to respond to the suggestions made by fact-finders and scientists. But there seems to be no doubt that in politics prestige is a decided factor. A poll of men whose biographies were included in *Who's Who* was used, for instance, in a political campaign some years ago to indicate that persons described as "superior and influential" were mainly on the side of one party and candidate. The prestige of businessmen has been a factor in political campaigns, especially in times of prosperity.

THE JAPS CALL IT "CO-PROSPERITY"

In wartime, belligerents stress the prestige of their military and political leadership. Sometimes this prestige is increased by legends, which are another means of influencing the attitudes of people. Usually legends are built up around a core of truth, but the end result may be like a character from fiction. The legends of Ulysses, Roland, and Siegfried, for example, grew up around mighty warriors. Whether legends are deliberately created or not, there can be no doubt that they are accepted and believed by many people, and so they influence the conduct of people. Someone has said that "masses of mankind live in these images" or legends.

MUSSOLINI WAS GOOD AT THROWING THE BULL . . . . BUT HE COULDN'T MAKE IT STICK

Hitler, Mussolini, and their followers have been industrious mythmakers. The near-deification of Hitler by the Nazis and the technique of mass hypnotism of the Germans are things that we, as a democratic people, find it very difficult to understand. To us it is incredible that a fanatical, intense, uneducated Munich agitator, unschooled in economics and politics, should be exalted by mass appeals and terroristic tactics into an all-powerful and "infallible" leader, "Der Führer," who exacts unquestioned obedience from his people. This "infallibility" that the Nazis have credited to Hitler is bluntly expressed in the words of Robert Ley, the director of the Nazi Labor Front. "Germany must obey like a well-trained soldier," he said. "The Führer, Adolf Hitler, is always right."

Why did large sections of the German public come to accept this legend of the Munich agitator? One historian thinks that it was because millions of Germans were yearning for "an end of all thought, will, or action on their own part in the conduct of their own affairs." The idea of a Führer, he believes, expressed their satisfaction in having found a leader who to them was "a symbol of absolute authority, a Great Father, a patriarch-ruler who can he worshipped as an all-wise Messiah, bringing solace and salvation to his sorely tried children." Hitler took "all responsibility for their own welfare." What they had to do was to give him "implicit faith and blind subordination."

SOME LIMITATIONS OF PROPAGANDA

While propaganda, using the tools of suggestion and persuasion, can gain important and significant objectives, it is a common mistake to overvalue its power. Men and women are not so easily swayed as some who fear propaganda seem to think.

There must be a reasonably fertile field to nourish the propagandist's seed before it can be expected to ripen into attitudes and opinions.

As one writer has pointed out, if the propaganda is not in harmony with the individual and his desire, it is likely to be met by cynical skepticism. The propaganda of Hitler, for example, fitted in with a German desire for supremacy; and the propaganda of the sellers of some patent medicine, whatever its real merits, harmonizes with the desire of people for good health.

Moreover, it should be remembered that forces quite apart from propaganda may have a large part in preparing the ground. One must be careful to distinguish between the opinion that *propaganda* creates and the opinion that is developed by *events*.

To give an illustration, the American attitude toward Germany was not bitterly hostile in the early months of World War I. But when the *Lusitania* was torpedoed in May 1915, with loss of 128 American lives, anger against the Central Powers mushroomed overnight.

The studies of George Gallup, since World War II started, reveal a similar relation between events and attitudes. In the early spring of 1940 only 7 Americans out of 100 voted "yes" in response to Dr. Gallup's question as to whether the United States should declare war on Germany. A month later, after the battle of Flanders, 16 out of 100 said they would vote for war if a national referendum were called. Dr. Gallup went on to say that "events and actions are infinitely more potent factors in influencing the formation of public opinion than a mere desire (for example) to imitate one's fellow citizens."

Goebbels' job as a propagandist was comparatively easy while the German armies were winning victories in Poland, the Low Countries, France, Norway, and Greece. But his job was not so easy after the tide began to turn. The routing of Rommel in North Africa, the invasion of Sicily and Italy, the smashing defeats of the Germans in Russia, the bombing of German cities, and the invasion on the west made the propaganda appeals of Goebbels far less effective in their impact than they had been before. It was only *after* Allied bombing of the Reich got into full swing that we began to hear of "weakening German morale."

No American should need to be reminded that the isolationists lost most of their following — and a good deal of their own conviction — within a matter of hours after the Japanese attack on Pearl Harbor.

Heredity and environment are also important in forming opinions, A great many men and women hold to the political beliefs of

their fathers. The public opinion polling
experts believe that sex, age, place of res-
idence, and income are all of some importance in influencing attitudes, and that on
some issues, race, religion, and party affilia-
tions also enter.

In addition to all these things, a man's own
knowledge and information may cause him to
hold to an opinion no matter how heavy the
barrage of propaganda attempting to force
him to change it.

So propaganda is not the all-powerful
weapon that many people believe it to be.
It is only one of the tools in the formation
of public opinion.

NEWS AND PROPAGANDA

While it is a serious mistake, as has been said, to overvalue propaganda, it is an equally serious mistake to assume, as some people do, that everything in the newspapers and on the radio, in the movies and magazines, is "propaganda"—propaganda that is self-seeking, deceitful, or otherwise improperly motivated. This is absurd.

The channels of communication can, of course, be used for propaganda. They can be used for "bad" propaganda and they can also be used for "good" propaganda. And they can be utilized for material that is not propaganda at all.

Let's look at just one case — that of the newspaper. Under the Constitution, freedom of the press is guaranteed. Why? Because a democratic nation knows that free expression of opinion and the free flow of facts, unhampered by governmental restrictions, is fundamental to intelligent action on the part of its citizens — and is also a social safety valve.

The journalist of today has a responsibility to *report facts* as accurately, objectively, and disinterestedly as is humanly possible. The newspaperman who respects himself and his work — the average newspaperman — accepts this responsibility. The honest, self-disciplined, well-trained reporter seeks to be a propagandist for nothing but the truth.

Of course propaganda does get into the press. Sometimes it is presented in the guise of impartial fact because the newspaperman is not sufficiently trained — or smart enough — to recognize it for what it is. Sometimes the newspaper is a conscious propagandist — in news and headlines both. And sometimes propaganda is so obviously news, and so obviously a matter of importance to the newspaper's readers, that the paper presents it knowing that the readers themselves will recognize it for what it is and evaluate it for themselves.

All this imposes a responsibility upon the newspaper reader, and it is with him that the responsibility of judgment ultimately should and does lie. The good newspaper-man does his best to confirm the news, to weed out propaganda that isn't news, and to present whatever propaganda the citizenry ought to know about. Having done that, he leaves it up to the reader for evaluation and criticism. He knows that the critical reader — one decently supplied with facts and having some knowledge of propaganda methods and purposes — can do his own job of separating the wheat from the straw, the important from the unimportant. That is the citizen's responsibility and his privilege in a democratic society.

DEFINING PROPAGANDA

While most persons who give the matter a thought make distinctions between an objec-tively written news report and propaganda, they encounter difficulty when they try to define propaganda. It is one of the most troublesome words in the English language. To define it clearly and precisely, so that whenever it is used it will mean the same thing to everybody, is like trying to get your hands on an eel. You think you've got it — then it slips away.

When you say "policeman" or "house," everybody has a pretty clear idea of what you mean. There's nothing vague about these terms, But when you try to mark off the exact boundaries of "propaganda," you wrinkle the brows even of the men who spend their lives studying the origin and history of words. And the problem of defining propaganda is all the more tangled because in the first World War it acquired certain popular meanings that stick to it like burrs to a cocker spaniel.

To some speakers and writers, propaganda is an instrument of the devil. They look on the propagandist as a person who is deliberately trying to hoodwink us, who uses half-truths, who lies, who suppresses, conceals, and distorts the facts. According to this idea of the word, the propagandist plays us for suckers.

Others think especially of techniques, of slogans, catchwords, and other devices, when they talk about propaganda. Still others define propaganda as a narrowly selfish attempt to get people to accept ideas and beliefs, always in the interest of a particular person or group and with little or no advantage to the public. According to this view, propaganda is promotion that seeks "bad" ends, whereas similar effort on behalf of the public and for "good" ends isn't propaganda, but is something else. Under this definition, for example, the writings of the patriotic Sam Adams on behalf of the American Revolution could not be regarded by American historians as propaganda.

The difficulty with such a view is that welfare groups and governments themselves secure benefits for a people through propaganda. Moreover, national propaganda in the throes of a war is aimed to bolster the security of the nonaggressor state and to assure the eventual well-being and safety of its citizens. No one would deny that this kind of propaganda, intelligently administered, benefits every man, woman, and child in the land.

The experts have plenty of trouble in agreeing upon a satisfactory definition of propaganda, but they are agreed that the term can't be limited to the type of propaganda that seeks to achieve bad ends or to the form that makes use of deceitful methods.

Can you distinguish propaganda from other forms of expression or promotion by saying that it is something that depends upon "concealment" — on hiding either the goals men are working for, or the means that they use, or the identity of the people behind the propaganda? A few authorities say "yes" to this question, but most of them say "no." Most analysts of propaganda do not limit the term propaganda to "veiled" promotion. Nor do they think it accurate to describe propaganda as an activity that resorts only to half-truths and downright falsehood. They say simply that some propaganda hinges on deceit and some does not. As a matter of fact, they recognize that a shrewd propagandist prefers to deal above the table, knowing just what the reaction

**GOEBBELS' JOB GOT TOUGHER WHEN
BOMBS BEGAN TO RAIN ON THE REICH**

of a propaganda-conscious public will be to dishonest trickery when it is exposed.

Some people limit the term propaganda to efforts that make use of emotional appeals, but others will differ about this idea. In a campaign to capture public opinion, a propagandist may rely heavily upon emotional symbols — but he may appeal to logical thinking as well.

Some people assert that propaganda is present only in controversial situations. One writer, for example, says, "Propaganda is an instrument of conflict or controversy, deliberately used." And another says, "If the report is deliberately circulated to influence

attitudes on controversial issues it is propaganda." When existing loyalties, customs,
and institutions are attacked, there is controversy. In a democratic system, propaganda replaces violence and censorship as
a method of bringing about change. All this
may be granted, and yet the question can be
raised whether the word "propaganda" should
be limited to efforts to influence attitudes on
controversial matters only.

Take, for example, the campaign in the
United States, conducted under the direc-
tion of the Surgeon General, for the control, cure, and eradication of venereal dis-
ease. This systematically organized campaign
tried to gain its ends by direct appeals to
the people. Those who handled it considered carefully just what agencies to use in
reaching the people — whether newspapers or
magazines, the radio or the public platform,
or a combination of these. They used both
emotional and logical appeals. They planned
the campaign to persuade diseased persons
to decide to visit a physician to get cured.
Their campaign used the techniques of propaganda, persuaded persons to a course
of conduct, and promised a reward — good
health. It used, as has been said, both emotional and logical appeals.

Unless "controversy" is interpreted to
include minor debates and the making of
choices in matters that command general
social approval, a definition of "propaganda"

that insists on stressing controversy hampers one's approach to an understanding of the subject.

All this will indicate that there is a lot of difficulty in working out any formal definition of propaganda. Most students of the subject agree that propaganda has to do with any ideas and beliefs that are intentionally propagated. They agree also that it attempts to reach a goal by making use of words and word substitutes (pictures, drawings, graphs, exhibits, parades, songs, and similar devices). Moreover, although it is used in controversial situations, most experts agree that it is also used to promote noncontroversial, or generally acceptable, ideas. Types of propaganda range from the selfish, deceitful, and subversive to the honest and aboveboard promotional effort. It can be concealed or open, emotional or containing appeals to reason, or a combination of emotional and logical appeals.

While propaganda influences the behavior of individuals, it is important to bear in mind that it is only one of the means by which man's behavior is influenced. There are other forms of inducement employed in winning assent or compliance. In limited or wholesale degree, depending upon the political organization of a given country, men have used force or violence to control people. They have resorted to boycott, bribery, passive resistance, and other techniques. Bribes, bullets, and bread have been called symbols of some of the actions that men have taken to force people into particular patterns of behavior.

Whatever propaganda may be, it differs from such techniques because it resorts to suggestion and persuasion.

HOW TO SIZE UP PROPAGANDA

No matter how we define it, the principal point on propaganda is this: *Don't be afraid of it.*

A few years ago this caution was more necessary than it is now. Propaganda was National Bogeyman No. 1. Speakers and writers saw magic in it. Some of them told us that we did everything but go to bed at night for no better reason than that the propagandist told us to. And so a great many people assumed that a propagandist was lurking behind every billboard, ready to spring out on us, and that whatever he told us was against our best interests.

Both of these ideas were incorrect. One fact that has been emphasized in this pamphlet is that much propaganda is "good." It urges us to do things that are for our own benefit. And another fact of importance is that much has been called propaganda when it has actually no promotional effort of any kind behind it.

In a democratic country, where free expression is basic, no one who thinks the matter through could possibly want to stamp out all propaganda. The essence of democracy is that rival points of view have the right to compete in the open. Decisions on political and other questions must be made by a free people. That means a people who don't shut their eyes and ears to opposing arguments, but instead look at them all, evaluate them, and throw out the ones that don't hold water.

1915—THE LUSITANIA

Events are often more important in crystallizing people's thoughts than is propaganda.

Those who spread an unreasoned fear of propaganda base their preachments on the unscientific notion that propaganda by itself governs public opinion. But the truth is that propaganda is only one of the factors that influence public opinion. *Specific information and sound knowledge of facts, presented without any propagandistic motive whatsoever, constitute an extremely important factor in the formation of public opinion.* Events, as we have seen, constitute another very important factor. And there are others. The wave of unreasoned fear of propaganda has somewhat leveled off. We clearly realize that, although some promotional campaigns have been conspicuously successful, others have been just as conspicuously failures—evidence that many factors, working together, influence and shape public opinion.

1941—PEARL HARBOR

The propaganda against propaganda confused many citizens and led them to ask, "What *can* I believe?" One writer, answering this question, says that "you can believe in yourself, your own common sense, your own decent instincts, your own values and traditions." The democratic principle requires that we come to our own judgments on the issues we face. Nobody can dodge the necessity of making up his own mind on any given question that calls for decision, whether it is international policy, local politics, or even the selection of one toothpaste over another. In making up his own mind he can look at all the propagandas and also bring into play all the information that is to be found outside propaganda and use every standard and criterion available to him in weighing values.

He should not forget that there are safeguards and checks for sizing up the merits of propaganda and the self-interest that may lie back of it. One authority on propaganda suggests two tests:

1. Is it really propaganda? Is some individual or group consciously trying to influence opinion and action? Who? For what purpose?

2. Is it true? Does a comparison of independent reports show that the facts are accurate? Does such a comparison show that the suggestions made are soundly based?

There are other tests that can be applied by the thinking citizen:

Which fact or set of facts in a piece of promotion are really important and relevant? Which are irrelevant?

If some individual or group is trying to influence opinion and action, is the effort selfish or is it unselfish? Will action resulting from the propaganda benefit the individual or group responsible for it? Or will it benefit those who act upon the suggestion given in the propaganda? Or will it benefit both?

HOW MANY PROPAGANDA IDEAS CAN YOU FIND IN THIS PICTURE?

What is likely to be the effect of the action or of the opinion that the propaganda is trying to set in motion?

All these points boil down to some very simple questions: What is the source of the propaganda? What is its authority? What purposes prompted it? Whom will it benefit? What does it really say?

TO THE LEADER

THERE HAS BEEN MUCH LOOSE talk about propaganda. This talk started long before the war. So-called educational campaigns of some commercial advertisers created suspicions in the minds of the public. Nazi use of propaganda before and during the war built up fear of it. But the fear evaporates, when people on the receiving end recognize what they read or hear for what it is. Witness the reception accorded Lord Haw-Haw in Britain.

Wide discussion of the question "What is propaganda?" will inoculate our citizens against the effects desired by the enemies of democracy. In a society which guards the right to freedom of speech, it is doubly important that people discriminate between legitimate talk about controversial issues and the type of propaganda that conceals fact and reason in a cloud of prejudice and fear. You will find one or more discussions or a forum on *What Is Propaganda?* useful in your program.

What Is Propaganda? can be particularly well handled in informal or panel discussion.

A forum or a symposium will be successful if your speakers are skillful and well informed. For suggestions on how to conduct discussion meetings, refer to War Department Education Manual, EM 1. *G. I. Roundtable: Guide for Discussion Leaders.*

Make *What Is Propaganda?* available, if possible, for reading by members of your group. Several individuals can share one copy if you will place those you have in a library, day room, service club, or other central spot for reading. Discussions go off better when members have some information upon which to base their talk. If you have an insufficient supply of the pamphlet for general reading by your group, be sure to spend, or have some assistant of yours use, the first five or ten minutes of the meeting for an introductory talk. In this introduction it would be important to attempt a definition of propaganda, suggesting the question whether a propagandist, in order to be such, must have a conscious purpose. You might raise here the issue of whether there is such a thing as good propaganda. You could mention some of the devices used by propagandists who seek to befog rather than clarify issues.

After the brief background talk you will need to have in mind some questions to get your group started. The questions that follow have been devised to suggest, but not to impose a procedure for the discussion:

FIRST — Develop a definition of propaganda. For many persons "propaganda" is a smear word, carrying the suggestion that anything to which it is applied is "bad." Is this too limited a meaning of the word? One writer on the subject says: "Propaganda is the *premeditated* selection of what we see and hear, designed to influence our attitudes." Is there such a thing as *unpremeditated* propaganda? Are all forms of propaganda "concealed," or are some open and avowed? Can propaganda be used in the public interest? Is it a phenomenon of recent origin? Why has it played such an important part in human history? Would you wish to stamp out all propaganda?

SECOND—Get your group to distinguish between propaganda and education. Are teachers propagandists? Are parents propagandists? Does the attitude of the propagandist differ from that of the scientist? How are the opinions of the average person formed? By newspaper, radio, or movies? Is it the function of education to train individuals to be immune to the distortions, the biases, the omissions, and the prejudices found in the various types of propaganda material? Is it the function of any other agency?

THIRD—Discuss this question: Are there differences between the use of propaganda in a democracy and in an authoritarian nation? Is advertising propaganda? What are the objectives of war propaganda? Of Nazi propaganda one expert says: "Nazi propaganda techniques include no secret devices, no newly-discovered psychological processes, no new channels of communication." If you support this statement, what *is* new about the Nazi method and why has it been so effective? Why, with all the amazing propaganda apparatus at his disposal, did Hitler think it necessary to use force against minority groups in the German nation?

FOURTH — Consider the safeguards against propaganda. Do specific information and a sound knowledge of facts influence opinion? What are some of the propaganda devices commonly used? What is a symbol? What is legend making? What is a slogan? How does the element of prestige work in fixing or altering attitudes and opinions? Do most persons accept such propagandas as seem most nearly to conform to their own interests, needs, and prejudices? Are most persons so "fed up" with propaganda that they do not let it affect them? Do many individuals support propaganda which is in the public interest and not solely in line with their own selfish interests? What propaganda devices did the Nazis "think up" to win followers? To "soften up" a nation they wished to absorb or attack? Do you believe this is a sound statement: "Although propaganda is pervasive and will be persistent, it need not be fatal to intelligent popular decisions"? Why do you believe or disbelieve the last statement?

A FEW SUGGESTIONS
FOR FURTHER READING
ABOUT PROPAGANDA

RADIO IN WARTIME. By Charles A. Siepmann. No. 26 of *America in a World at War*, published by the Oxford University Press, 114 Fifth Avenue, New York, N.Y. (1942).

WAR IN THE TWENTIETH CENTURY. Edited by Willard Waller. Published by the Dryden Press, 103 Park Avenue, New York, N.Y. (1940). See the chapter entitled "Propaganda and Public Opinion" by Ralph D. Carey.

RADIO GOES TO WAR: THE "FOURTH FRONT." By Charles J. Rolo. Published by G. P. Putnam's Sons, 2 West 45th Street, New York 19, N.Y. (1940).

DEMOCRACY THROUGH PUBLIC OPINION. By Harold D. Lasswell. Published by George Banta Publishing Company, 150 Ahnaip Street, Menasha, Wisconsin (1911),

AN INTRODUCTION TO PUBLIC OPINION, By Harwood L. Childs, Published by John Wiley and Sons, 440 Fourth Avenue, New York, N.Y. (1910).

THE STRATEGY OF TERROR: EUROPE'S INNER FRONT. By Edmond Taylor. Published by Houghton Mifflin Company, 2 Park Street, Boston 7, Massachusetts (1940).

NEWS IS A WEAPON. By Matthew Gordon. Published by Alfred A. Knopf, 501 Madison Avenue, New York 22, N.Y. (1942).

CONQUERING THE MAN IN THE STREET. By Ellis Freeman. Published by the Vanguard Press, 424 Madison Avenue, New York, N.Y. (1940).

MOBILIZING FOR CHAOS: THE STORY OF THE NEW PROPAGANDA. By Oscar W. Riegel. Published by Yale University Press, New Haven, Connecticut (1934).

PUBLIC OPINION. By William Albig. Published by McGraw-Hill Book Company, 330 West 42nd Street, New York, N.Y. (1939). See especially chapters 17 and 18.

POLITICAL PROPAGANDA. By Frederic C. Bartlett. Published by the Cambridge University Press (1940). Distributed by Macmillan Company. 60 Fifth Avenue, New York 11, N.Y.

THE FINE ART OF PROPAGANDA. Edited by Alfred M. Lee and Elizebeth B. Lee for the Institute for Propaganda Analysis, Inc. Published by Harcourt, Brace and Company, 383 Madison Avenue, New York 17, N.Y. (1939).

WELL, WHAT *IS* PROPAGANDA?